X-TREME
LATIN

X-TREME LATIN

LINGUA LATINA EXTREMA

All the Latin you need to
know for surviving
the 21st century

HENRY BEARD
HENRICUS BARBATUS

headline

First published in 2004 by
Gotham Books, a division of Penguin Group (USA) Inc.

First published in Great Britain in 2004 by
HEADLINE BOOK PUBLISHING

10 9 8 7 6 5 4 3

Cataloguing in Publication Data is available from the British Library

ISBN 0 7553 1295 3

Illustrations by Valerie Baker

Designed by Viv Mullett

Typeset in Dante MT by Avon DataSet Ltd, Bidford-on-Avon, Warks
Printed and bound in Great Britain by
Clays Ltd St Ives plc

Headline's policy is to use papers that are natural, renewable and recyclable
products and made from wood grown in sustainable forests. The logging and
manufacturing processes are expected to conform to the environmental
regulations of the country of origin.

HEADLINE BOOK PUBLISHING
A division of Hodder Headline
338 Euston Road
London NW1 3BH

www.headline.co.uk
www.hodderheadline.com

Contents
INDEX CAPITUM

II. INTERMEDIATE LATIN

III. ADVANCED LATIN

Author's Note

Although I did the original Latin composition for the first draft of this book, my translations have been extensively corrected, meticulously polished, and felicitously rephrased by J. Mark Sugars, Ph.D., without whose assistance I would have been in *merda profundissima* (very deep doo-doo). Thus, to the extent that the classical constructions herein are historically appropriate, grammatically accurate, and culturally apt, it is he who deserves the imposing, but tasteful, triumphal arch on the sunny side of the Forum, just below the Palatine Hill. If, however, there are any *errata ignominiosa* (cock ups), it is I and I alone who should be exiled to the remote, windswept tip of some godforsaken island inhabited by rude barbarians. (The Hamptons will do nicely.)

That said, I have to confess that even the most dedicated Latin purist inevitably succumbs to the temptation to make a cheap joke at the expense of the noble tongue of Rome's golden age, and I am no exception. Therefore, in the interests of scholarly integrity, I am compelled to concede that there is no Latin verb *'geronimo, geronimare'* meaning 'to express an intention to act boldly or rashly,' say, just prior to jumping off a bridge, and if a Roman diner wished to remark, 'I will recommend this restaurant,' *'zago, zagas, zagat'* is not the way he would have phrased it. The rest of the Augustan yadda-yadda (*'iaddo, iaddere, iaddedi, iadditum'*) is as kosher as we could make it.

Oh, all right. Yadda-yadda is actually *blatero, blaterare.* Sheesh.

Preface
PRAEFATIO
PRY-FAH-TIH-OH

It's often said that Latin is a dead language
Lingua Latina saepe dicitur mortua esse
LEEN-gwah lah-TEE-nah SIGH-pay DEE-kih-tuhr MOHR-too-ah EHS-seh

Bollocks!
Coleus!
Koh-LEE-uhs!

It's just been taking a long nap
Modum iam pridem meridiatur
MOH-duhm yahm PREE-dehm meh-ree-dih-AH-tuhr

And it's been talking a lot in its sleep
Iam diu autem multa verba facit dormiens
Yahm DIH-ooh OW-tehm MOOL-tah WEHR-bah FAH-kiht DOHR-mih-ehns

In fact, you can't get it to shut up
Re vera, non potes eam in silentium redigere
Ray WAY-rah nohn POH-tess EH-ahm ihn sih-LAYN-tih-uhm reh-DIHG-eh-reh

Look around – Latin is all over the place, like a cheap toga
Circumspice – Lingua Latina se pandit ubique tanquam toga vilis
KEER-kuhm-spih-keh – LEEN-gwah lah-TEE-nah say PAHN-diht ooh-BEE-kweh TAHN-kwaum TOH-gah WIH-liss

Lawyers use it to screw you
Iurisperiti ea utuntur ut te defraudent
Yoo-riss-peh-REE-tee EH-ah uh-TOON-tuhr uht tay deh-FROW-dehnt

Doctors use it to scare you shitless
Medici hac lingua utuntur ut alvum evacues ex metu
MEH-dih-kee hock LEEN-gwah uh-TOON-tuhr uht AHL-wuhm ay-WAH-koo-ays eks MEH-tooh

Politicians use it to hide their tracks while they rob you blind
Magistratus ea utuntur ad operienda vestigia cum te despoliant
Mah-gihs-TRAH-toohs EH-ah uh-TOON-tuhr ahd oh-pehr-ih-AYN-dah wehs-TEE-gih-ah kuhm tay deh-SPOH-lih-ahnt

Priests use it to weasel their way out when they get caught playing hide-the-sausage with the altar boys
Sacerdotes in stupro cum acolytis deprehensi ea utuntur ut se criminibus absolvant
Sah-kehr-DOH-tays ihn STOOP-roh kuhm ah-koh-LEE-teese day-preh-HAYN-see EH-ah uh-TOON-tuhr uht say krih-MIHN-ih-buhss ahb-SOHL-wahnt

Even garden supply stores use it to get you to buy
overpriced, short-lived houseplants

**Etiam venditores rerum hortensium ea utuntur ad
persuadendum tibi ut emas maximo pretio plantas
vitae brevis**

*EH-tih-ahm wehn-dih-TOHR-ace RAY-ruhm hohr-TAYN-sih-
uhm EH-ah uh-TOON-tuhr ahd pehr-swah-DAYN-duhm TIH-
bee uht EH-mahs MAHK-sih-moh PREH-tih-oh PLAHN-tahs
WEE-tye BREH-wihss*

The fact is, for too long these dirtbags have had a
monopoly on this mighty tongue

**Diutius quidem haec propudia monopolio huius
magnifici sermonis fruuntur**

*Dih-OO-tih-uhs KWIH-dehm hike proh-POOH-dih-ah moh-
noh-POH-lih-oh HOO-eeh-uhss mahg-NIH-fih-kee sehr-MOH-
nihss frooh-OON-tuhr*

But now, thanks to this little book, you too can tap the
awesome power of Latin to dismay the ignorant
multitudes

**Nunc vero, huius libelli gratia, tu quoque potentia
reverenda linguae Latinae uti potes ad indoctum
vulgus consternandum**

*Nuhnk WAY-roh, HOO-eeh-uhss lih-BEHL-lee GRAH-tih-ah,
too KWOH-kweh poh-TAYN-tih-ah reh-weh-RAYN-dah
LEEN-gwigh LAH-tih-nigh OO-tee POH-tehss ahd ihn-
DOHK-tuhm WUHL-guhs kohn-stehr-NAHN-duhm*

And best of all, you'll be able to insult and abuse one and
all in perfect safety, using a language that everyone
respects but practically no one understands

**Atque haec est optima ratio omnium: maledicere
cunctis hominibus et contumeliam imponere satis
impune poteris verbis augustis quae cum omnes
magno aestimant, tum nemo ferme intellegit**

*AHT-kweh hike ehst OHP-tih-mah RAH-tih-oh OHM-nih-uhm:
mah-leh-DEEK-eh-reh KOONK-tees hoh-MIHN-ih-buhss eht
kohn-tuh-MAY-lih-ahm ihm-POH-neh-reh SAH-tihss ihm-
POO-neh poh-TEH-rihss WAYR-beese ow-GOOS-teese kwy
kuhm OHM-nays MAHG-noh EYE-stih-mahnt tuhm NEH-mo
FAYR-meh ihn-TEHL-leh-giht*

And as you pepper your speech with catapult-powered
put-downs, remember the immortal words of Maximus
as he signaled the attack in Pannonia:

**Itaque cum spargis orationem tuam praepotentibus
opprobriis, memento verborum immortalium quae
Maximus fecit signum dans in Pannonia:**

*Ih-TAH-kweh kuhm SPAHR-ghiss oh-rah-tih-OH-nehm TOO-
ahm prigh-poh-TAYN-tih-buhss ohp-PROH-brih eehs, meh-
MEHN-toh wayr-BOH-ruhm ihm-mohr-TAH-lih-uhm kwigh
MAHK-sih-muhss FAY-kiht SIHG-nuhm dahns ihn Pahn-
NOH-nih-ah:*

Unleash hell!
Solve lora infernis!
SOHL-weh LOH-rah ihn-FEHR-nihss!

And have a nice day!
Et futue te ipsum!
Eht FUH-too-eh tay IHP-suhm

Latin Terms in Modern English

LEGAL LATIN

Latin word or phrase	*English meaning*
in flagrante delicto	
habeas corpus	
prima facie	you're in big trouble
nolo contendere	
res ipsa loquitur	

MEDICAL LATIN

Latin word or phrase	*English meaning*
macula	
fistula	
carcinoma	you're dead
angina	
medulla oblongata	

POLITICAL LATIN

Latin word or phrase	*English meaning*
pro forma	
ex officio	
per diem	the fix is in
sine qua non	
quid pro quo	

ECCLESIASTICAL LATIN

Latin word or phrase	*English meaning*
ex cathedra	
in pectore	
urbi et orbi	the bishop is not
in hoc signo vinces	available
sic transit gloria mundi	

BOTANICAL LATIN

Latin word or phrase	*English meaning*
grandiflora	
tomentosa	leafless clump of dry
pendula	brown twigs in one
rugosa	week flat
sempervirens	

Basic Latin Pronunciation Guide

VOWELS

a   if long, as in 'bl*ah*'; if short, as in 'rub-*a*-dub'
e   if long, as in 'ol*é*'; if short as in 'f*eh*'
i   if long, as in ''z*i*ne'; if short as in 'z*i*t'
o   if long, as in 'd'*oh*'; if short as in 'n*o*t'
u   if long, as in 'd*u*de'; if short as in 'wass*u*p'

There is really no simple way to tell if a vowel is long or short, but if the word is short – one syllable – treat the vowel as short. The last syllable of verb endings are almost always short. If *a, i, o,* or *u,* come at the end of a word, they're long; if *e* comes at the end of a word, it's short. If a vowel is followed by two consonants, it's long. For other situations, pronuntia utrolibet modo! (wing it!)

DIPTHONGS

ae   as in 'Th*ai*'
au   as in '*ou*ch'
ei   as in 'h*ey*'
eu   as in 'h*ey*, y*ou*'
oe   as in 'g*oy*'
ui   as in 'pt*ui*'

CONSONANTS

b, d, f, h, I, m, n, and *p* are the same as in English. So are *k* and *z*, which are rare in Latin anyway. *j, w,* and the consonant *y* don't exist in Latin.

c, ch   always 'k.' That's a KIGH-sahr salad you ordered. You want ANN-koh-veese with that?

g, gn   always 'guh.' The Romans were fighting the GUHR-mahns, not the JUR-mahns, and when they gave the signal to attack, it was a SIHG-nuhm (trumpet blast) not a SEE-nuhm (large bowl).

i   always 'yuh.' It's thanks to YOO-lih-uhss (not JOO-lee-yuss) that we celebrate the fourth of July instead of the fourth of Quinctil.

r   you can rrroll your r's even if they'rrre the last letterrr of a worrrrd.

s   always 'sss.' The Roman fanss (not fanz) were animalss (not animalz).

t, th   always 'teh.' Teh-hey teh-rew teh-hings at eak otteh-her during teh-he nah-tih-oh-nahl (not nashunal) ant-hem (not anthum).

v   always 'w.' The wolcano that waporized Pompeii was Weh-SOO-wee-uhss.

There are no silent letters in Latin – every vowel (unless it's part of a two-syllable dipthong) and every consonant is always pronounced fully, and often separately. Of course, there are also no actual Romans around to sneer when you mess up.

A Little Story
NARRATIUNCULA

Puellae filiae agricolarum sunt
The girls are the daughters of the farmers

Puellae pulchrae sunt
The girls are pretty

Puellae nautas in via spectant
The girls see the sailors in the street

Nautae pulchri sunt
The sailors are hunks

Puellae nautas salutant
The girls say hello to the sailors

O malam fortunam! Nautae male mares sunt
Too bad! The sailors are homos

Nautae ad puellas digitos impudicos porrigunt
The sailors give the girls the finger

Puellae nautas appellant
The girls call out to the sailors

'Speramus naviculam misellam vestram ad scopulum
   adlisam iri summersum'
'We hope your stupid boat hits a rock and sinks'

Puellae in forum descendere destinant et ibi
   mercimonium furari
**The girls decide to go down to the mall and shoplift
some stuff**

Omnes paucis annis prosedae erunt
In a few years they will all be hookers

Latin Aptitude Test
PROBATIO LATINITATIS

(answers below – *responsa recta in ima pagina*)

I. MATH – SCIENTIA MATHEMATICA

All Gaul is divided into ___ parts
Gallia est omnis divisa in partes ___

A. many
   multas
B. good
   bonas
C. small
   parvas
D. warlike
   bellicosas
E. Capture a Gaul and torture him until he tells you
   Torque Gallum captum donec tibi respondeat

II. VERBAL – SCIENTIA VERBORUM

Arms and the man I sing, who first from the shores of
___ . . .
Arma virumque cano ___ qui primus ab oris . . .

A. Syracuse
   Syracusarum
B. Ithaca
   Ithacae
C. Albany
   Albani
D. Buffalo
   Bufali
E. Sacrifice a bullock to Jupiter so the test gets canceled
   because the teacher was struck by lightning
   *Immola Iovi iuvencum ut magistro tacto de caelo probatio
   relinquatur*

III. EXTRA CREDIT – QUAESTIO ADDITA PRAEMII GRATIA

Whatever it is, I fear the Greeks even when bearing
_____

Quidquid id est, timeo Danaos et _____ ferentes

A. shish kebabs
   carunculas veribus fixas
B. stuffed grape leaves
   folia vitis oryza farta
C. baklava
   crustula laminosa
D. the check
   syngrapham
E. Send a slave over later with the answer, and if he gets it
   wrong, lop off his ears
   *Mitte brevi postea servum qui responsum referat atque si
   erret praecide aures ei*

I., E; II, E; III, E.

Romulus and Remus Jokes
ROMULI REMIQUE IOCULARIA

ROMULUS: Why did the sacred chicken cross the Appian Way?

ROMULUS: Quem ob rem pullus sacer viam Appiam transivit?

REMUS: I do not know. Let us cut it open and see if the entrails provide an explanation for this inauspicious behaviour!

REMUS: Nescio. Eum evisceremus ut, extane ostensura sint illius infausti facti causam, comperiamus!

ROMULUS: Why do Roman firemen wear red braces?

ROMULUS: Cur gerunt siphonarii Romani retinacula rubra?

REMUS: I do not know – let us set the city ablaze and see if their trousers fall down!

REMUS: Nescio. Urbem incendamus ut, sintne delapsurae bracae eorum, comperiamus!

ROMULUS: Why did the Helvetian moron throw the water clock out the window?

ROMULUS: Quare iecit caudex Helvetius clepsydram de fenestra?

REMUS: I do not know, but I feel certain that after ten years chained to an oar as a galley slave he will be eager to reveal the reason for his rash act!

REMUS: Nescio; pro certo tamen habeo istum, decem annos vinctum in servitio ad remum intra navem longam, cupidum futurum revelare rationem sui temerarii facti!

The Legion of Superheroes
LEGIO HEROUM MAXIMORUM

Faster than a speeding chariot . . .
Celerior quam currus festinans . . .

More powerful than a Carthaginian war-elephant . . .
Valentior quam elephas bellicus Punicus . . .

Able to conjugate irregular verbs without making a single mistake . . .
Potis anomala verba sine lapsu declinare . . .

It's Ro-Man!
Romanus est!

T-shirt Slogans
TITULI TUNICALES

CARPE NAREM
Pick your nose

CAPE SOMNUM
Catch some 'z's'

CAPIAMUS CEREVISIAM
Let's grab a beer

CAVE LABOREM
Beware of work

MORANS FAC PAUSAM UT SEDES BIROTARUM
  OLFACIAS
Take time to stop and smell the bicycle seats

PUTEO ERGO SUM
I stink, therefore I am

VENI, VIDI, VOMUI
I came, I saw, I blew lunch

SOLVE LORA INFERNIS
Unleash hell

OSTENDE MIHI PECUNIAM
Show me the money

PARENTES MEI DIMIDIUM EUROPAE DESPOLIA
   VERUNT. EGO TAMEN NIL ACCEPI PRAETER
   HANC TUNICULAM MISELLAM
**My parents plundered half of Europe and all I got was
this stupid T-shirt**

ABES ETIAM A CONSILIO INSULTANDI MIHI NISI
   LATINE LOQUI SCIAS
Don't even think of dissing me unless you speak Latin

ILLUC IVI, ILLUD FECI
Been there, done that

Bumper Stickers
TITULI CURRULES

I'd rather be pillaging
Malim praedari

I'm dumb and I vote
Hebes sum et suffragia fero

My child can beat the crap out of your wimpy honor student
Filius meus puerum tuum studiosum laureatum mollem deverberare potest

Thank you for not thanking me for not smoking
Tibi gratias ago quod mihi gratias non agis quod fumum non comedo

Visualize world conquest
Habe ante oculos devictionem mundi

Keep honking – I'm reloading
Perge cornu canere – sclopetum repleo

Horn broken – watch for finger
Buccina fracta – exspecta signum digiti impudici

Barbarian on board
Barbarus in curru

Proud of our brutal police
Vigilitus nostris crudelibus gloriantes

Stop the aqueduct, save the unicorns
**Sistite constructionem aquaeductus ut conservetis
unicornes**

I brake for lunch
Frenos inhibere soleo pransurus

Don't blame me – I voted for Miss Piggy
Nolite me culpare – Suffragatus sum Erae Porcellae

Jesus loves you – everyone else thinks you're an asshole
Te amat Iesus – ceteri te putant irrumatorem

If you can read this, I lost my trailer
Si hoc potes legere, traheam meam amisi

Reality TV
SPECTACULA TELEVISORIA
VERI SIMILIA

Celebrity Shark Attack
Impetus Pistricum in Insignes

Supermodel Food Fight
Pulcherrimae Inter Se Luctantes Edulibus

Beach Babe Lapdance Showdown
Certamen Ultimum Saltandi Nympharum Litoralium in Genibus Virorum

Blow Job Island
Insula Fellatoria

Nationwide Red Alert Hot Bod Strip Search
Inquisitio Summa Cum Vigilantia Per Omnes Nationis Partes Diffusa Corporum Formosiorum Nudatorum

Meet the Organ Donors
Salvete, O Daturi Membra Post Mortem

Baby-sitters from Hell Bring Home Animals that Kill for Fun
Nutriculae Infernales in Domos Adducunt Feras Quae ad Delicias Interficiunt

Big Fat Slobs Eat Shit for Cash
Helluones Squalidi Merdam Pro Nummis Comedunt

Who Wants to Marry a Rich Old Fart with a Terminal
Disease?
Quis Vult Nubere Peditori Capulari Diviti?

Hardball Talk Shows
DISCEPTATIONES TUMULTUOSAE

That's a load of bull, and you know it!
Merae fabulae sunt, et eas esse tales scis!

You wouldn't know a fact if one hit you on the head!
Rem veram non cognoscas etiamsi frontem tibi feriat!

You're a liberal stooge!
Pedisequus parasiticus es popularium!

You're a right-wing moron!
Stipator stultus es optimatum!

See you next week!
Vos revisemus post septimanam!

Ultimate Sports
LUDI EXTRAORDINARII

Bass-fishing – Piscatus Percarum

Let me guess – you have to drink the beer to make room
in the ice chest for all the fish you catch
**Ut coniecturam faciam – necesse est tibi bibere
cerevisiam ut locum in cista glaciei des piscibus captis**

It's a keeper!
Licet mihi hunc retinere!

Stock car racing – Certamen Curruum Generalium

When are they going to start running into each other and
blowing up?
**Quando inter se collidentes incipient in flammas
dirumpi?**

Pit stop!
Statio restaurativa!

Wrestling – Luctatus

Something tells me that the mean-looking bearded guy dressed up like the Ayatollah is no match for the wily Captain America

Suspicor illum truculentum barbatum ritu archierei Persici vestitum non esse comparem Centurioni Americano vafro

Smashmouth! Smackdown!
Ictus in os! Prostratio!

Bungee jumping – Saltus de Ponte

How dumb would you have to be to jump off a bridge with a rope tied to your foot?

Quam vecors sit is qui de ponte saliat pedibus funiculo ligatis?

Geronimo!
Geronimo, geronimare!

Snowboarding – Super Nivem Labi

Hey dude, let's head to the halfpipe, catch some major air, and stick some tricks!

Heus, laute, contendamus ad canalem nivalem ut aerem oppido capientes nonnullas technas exsequamur!

Super rad! I'm stoked!
Maxime radicitus! Flagro!

The Olympics – Olympia

I'll vote for the Greek in the wrestling if you vote for the
  Roman in the chariot race
**Graeco palmam dabo in certamine luctandi si Romano
  palmam dabis in certamine quadrigarum**

Deal!
Fiat haec pactio!

Trash Talk in the Colosseum
CONTUMELIA IN AMPHITHEATRO FLAVIO

You want a part of me? Bring it on!
Visne partem mei capere? Comminus agamus!

Are you dissing me?
Insultasne tu miki?

You're yesterday's news
In actis diurnis iamdudum es celebratus

You're toast
Mox corvos pasces

You don't know your ass from a catacomb
Non possis distinguere tuum podicem a Puticulis

Your mother is so fat, when she's in town, Rome has eight hills
Mater tua tam obesa est ut cum Romae est, urbs habet octo colles

Your mother is so ugly, when the gods turned her into a pig, she thought her prayers had been answered
Mater tua tam turpis est ut cum di eam mutaverint in porcam, suas preces putaverit eos audivisse

Your mother is so stupid, when she found a coin with
  Caesar's name on it, she tried to return it to him
**Mater tua tam stulta est ut cum invenerit nummum
  ferentem nomen Caesaris, huic eum restituere conata
  sit**

Go ahead, punk – make my day
Age, catamite – fac mihi hunc diem felicissimum

Spring Break
FERIAE VERNALES

Road trip!
Iter faciamus!

Let's party hearty!
Pergraecemur!

Wet T-shirt contest!
Certamen inter mammosas tunicis madefactis vestitas!

Go ahead, ask for proof of age. See, I've got a Latin ID.
  I'm 2,000 years old.
**Age, scrutare chartam identitatis meam. Ecce, est mihi
  syngraphus Latinus. Duo milia annorum sum natus.**

I'm wasted!
Crapulentus sum!

I'm going to throw up!
Vomiturus sum!

Country Music Favourites
MUSICA RUSTICA
FAVORABILISSIMA

Si Telephonium Non Tintinnat, Ego Voco
If Your Phone Doesn't Ring, It's Me

Causam Tibi Dabo Bibendi
I'll Give You Something to Drink About

Quomodo Una Nocte Facta Tam Turpis Es?
How Did You Get So Ugly Overnight?

Si Dies Hodiernus Esset Piscis, Reicerem
If Today Was a Fish I'd Throw it Back

Mater Cape Malleum, Musca Sedet in Capite Patris
Mother Get the Hammer, There's a Fly on Papa's Head

Si Me Deseras, Liceatne Mihi Te Comitari?
If You Leave Me, Can I Come Too?

Quomodo Te Desiderare Potero Si Non Discesseris?
How Can I Miss You If You Won't Go Away?

Per Anulum Illa Trusit Digitum Medicinalem, Ac Ostendit
  Mihi Digitum Medium
She Got the Ring, and I Got the Finger

Tu Causa Es Cur Liberi Nostri Tam Turpiculi Sint
You're the Reason Our Kids Are So Ugly

Sine Te Tam Miser Sum Ut Videaris Etiamnunc Adesse
**I'm So Miserable Without You It's Like Having You
Here**

Caput Dolet, Pedes Fetent, Iesum Non Amo
My Head Hurts, My Feet Stink, and I Don't Love Jesus

Chilling Out
SERMO OTIOSORUM

Wassup?
Quagis?

Nothin', watching the game
Nihil ago, ludos specto

True, true
Vero, vero

It's off the hook
Ab unco remotumst

Talk to the hand, the face don't understand
Adloquere manum, facies nescit quid velis

Black togas are cool
Togae atrae lepidae sunt

Want to see my sword collection?
Vin' aspicere collectum gladiorum meum?

I'm thinking of taking a catapult into the school
cafeteria . . .
Cogito ferre catapultam in cenationem scholae . . .

Graffiti
INSCRIPTIONES LATRINALES

Make love, not war – hell, get married, do both
Suscipite amorem, non bellum – eheu, iuncti matrimonio, suscipite utrumque

Procrastinate now
Procrastina rem nunc

Flush twice, it's a long way to Texas
Evacua cratera latrinalem bis, Texas procul est

If it has tits, tyres, or testicles, it's nothing but trouble
Mammeatae, rotalia, testiculati, omni modo molesta sunt

Gods are dead
Di mortui sunt

Beauty is in the eye of the beer-holder
Cervesia pota, pulchritudo cernitur

Yankee, go home – and take me with you
Americani, redite domum – ducentes me vobiscum

If we aren't supposed to eat animals, why are they made
   of meat?
**Si quidem animalia nobis edenda non sunt, quare
   constant ex carne?**

There are three kinds of people: those who can count,
   and those who can't
**Sunt genera tria hominum: illi qui numerare possunt,
   et illi qui non possunt**

It *is* as bad as you think, and they *are* out to get you
**Res tam malae sunt quam putas, et inimici re vera te
   persequuntur**

Why don't psychics ever win the lottery?
**In sortitionibus donativis, cur numquam praemia
   consequuntur sortilegi?**

Aunt Em: Hate you, Hate Kansas, Taking the dog –
   Dorothy
**Amita Aemilia: Te Kansiamque odi, Canem mecum
   abduco – Dorothea**

If walking is so good for you, why does my mailman look
   like Jabba the Hut?
**Si quidem pedibus ire tam salubre corpori est, cur
   similis est noster tabellarius forma illi Iabbae Hutico?**

Kill Barney
**Interfice Arcturulum, istum mimum personatum
   portentosum purpureum palaeozoicum**

Road Rage
IRA IN VIA

Where did you learn to drive – fleeing from Huns?
Ubi didicisti gubernare currum? In fuga ab Hunnis?

That's it, numbnuts. Pull out in front of me, then slow
down when you get to the light.
**Euge, enervate eunuche! Ingredere in orbitam meam
prae me, tum reprime cursum cum biviali lucernae
approprinquas.**
Now speed up when I try to pass you, and as I go by, give
me the finger
**Nunc, accelera cum conor te praeterire, mihique
praetereunti ostende digitum impudicum**

Okay, tailgater – time for a brake check
Em, ichneumon – tempus est sufflamina temptare

Big car, little dick
Currus magnus, mentula minuscula

You know what S.U.V.s and hemorrhoids have in
common? Every asshole has one.
**Scisne quid commune superlativa urbana vehicula cum
haemorrhoidis habeant? Est unum ex his utrisque
malis cuique pathico.**

Lady, if you're going to sit there all day yakking on your mobile, why don't you stick a steering wheel on your living room wall and just stay home?

Muliercula, si vis ibi sedens garrire totum diem in Nokiam tuam, quidni rotam adfigens gubernalem ad murum conclavis domi maneas?

What are you saving those pretty little turn signals for – Christmas?

Quod ad tempus reservas ista lumina pulchella praemonitoria – ad Saturnalia?

No, Mr Busybody, I am not handicapped, but you will be if you don't move your nosy butt out of that parking place, pronto

Minime, ardelio, nullo modo debilis sum, sed fies tu quidem, si clunes tuas curiosas non removeris protinam ab illa statione

Don't clamp my car!

Noli caligam in rotam currus mei adfigere!

I am too allowed in the car pool lane! See, I'm not alone. I suffer from multiple personality disorder.

Certe mihi licet vehi in orbita seposita curribus repletis. Ecce, non solus sum. Legio mihi nomen est, quia multi sumus.

There are three of us here. I want to drive! No, it's my turn! Not fair, what about me? Me me me!

Adsunt tres. Volo gubernare! Immo, ordo memet vocat! Iniquum est! Quid de me? Me me me!

Does that Breathalyzer have a Latin setting?
**Potestne illa machina pneumatodocimastica ad linguam
Latinam accommodari?**

I have Vatican diplomatic immunity. If you give me a
ticket, you're going to end up cooling your heels in The
Hague in a jail cell full of Yugoslavian war criminals.
**Sedes Romana Sacra mihi diplomaticam immunitatem
tribuit. Si me vocaveris in ius, aetatem tuam deges
Hagae Comitis, conditus in carcerem refertum
Iugoslavorum condemnatorum de bellum contra ius
gentium gerendo.**

Air Rage
IRA IN AËRE

Do you have nail-clipper-sniffing dogs?
Habetisne canes quae forficulas unguales olfacere possunt?

I think that guy with a napkin on his noggin has a catapult
in his shoe
**Credo illum mantelium in capite gerentem occultavisse
catapultam in caliga**

Hey, pal, is that carry-on luggage or did you just sack
Carthage?
**Heia, amice, utrum illae sunt sarcinae tuae, an modo
Carthaginem despoliasti?**

Say, miss, didn't you used to work for Con Air?
**Dic mihi, domnicella, nonne te conducebat aëria classis
quae condemnatos transportabat?**

You know, even galley slaves were served meals
Nempe cibus dabatur etiam servis navalibus

If there's an accident, I'm going to charge people to use
this exit
**Si de caelo cadere incipiamus, vectores pretium pro usu
huius exitus poscam**

Warning Labels
SCHEDAE MONITORIAE

Your nose may fall off
Fieri potest ut nasus tuus decidat

You may develop hot-dog fingers
Fieri potest ut digiti tui formam tomaculorum sumant

Your head may explode
Fieri potest ut caput tuum displodatur

Your brain may turn to mush
Fieri potest ut cerebrum tuum liquefiat

You may start babbling in Latin
Fieri potest ut Latine blaterare incipias

II
LINGUA LATINA
MEDIA

INTERMEDIATE LATIN

Caesar's PowerPoint Presentation
CAESAR TIBI PROPOSITA MAXIMI MOMENTI PRAEFERT

I

Argumentum	*Topic*
Gallia, terra in partes tres divisa	Gaul, a country with three parts
*Cisalpina	*Northern Italy
*Transalpina	*France
*Oblitus sum tertiae	*I forget

II

Consilium	*Plan*
*Visere	*Make a visit
*Videre	*Have a look-see
*Vincere	*Take it over

III

Sequelae	*Follow-up*
*De bello stultum librum scribam	*Write a stupid book about it
*A nonnullis irrumatoribus occidar in Foro	*Get assassinated in the forum by a bunch of assholes
*Acetaria et mensis accipient a me nomina	*Salad and month get named after me

IV

Conclusio	*Conclusions*
*Faciam ut animus meus scrutetur	*Get head examined
*Quid illa femella Cleopatra?	*What about that Cleopatra dame?

Top 10 Reasons to Live in the Time of the Caesars

DECEM OPTIMAE RATIONUM CUR IN AEVO CAESARUM VIVERE IUCUNDIUS ESSET

X. Calculus won't be invented for another fifteen hundred years
Calculus differentialis non invenietur intra mille quingentos annorum

IX. When you're late on a rainy day, you can always blame the sundial
Si sub love pluvioso serius advenias, tu culpare semper potes horologium solare

VIII. If you piss off one god, you've still got 600 left
Si deum irrites unum, sescenti tibi iam supersint

VII. Actors are treated like dirt
Histriones foede tractantur

VI. Athletes who complain about their pay end up in an urn
Athletae qui queruntur de mercedibus mox in urnas funduntur

V. Scumbags who get the death penalty think they got off light
Scelesti mortis damnati se leviores poenas pensuros reuntur

IV. The likeliest place to find some pushy Christian preacher is inside a lion
Veri simillimum est, locum in quo praedicatorem Christianum protervum invenies, ventrem leoninum esse

III. The French are an ignorant bunch of servile peasants living in smelly huts, and the Germans are getting their asses kicked
Gens Gallorum inerudita servilis agrestis est, in tuguriis foetidis habitans, et Germani vapulant

II. A healthy diet consists of waiting to see if the food taster dies before having anything to eat
Diaeta salubris est, antequam aliquid cenes, observare an moriatur praegustator

I. Everyone is always dressed for a toga party
Omnès amiciuntur semper togis quasi convivium agitaturi

That Old-Time Religion
ILLA RELIGIO PRISCA

Actually, I'm a born-again pagan
**Re vera, cultor denuo renatus deorum Romanorum
antiquorum sum**

I get to worship whomever I like, including SpongeBob
SquarePants
**Licet mihi venerari pro deo quemlibet, etiam
SpongoRobertum QuadratoBracatum**

I always ask myself, What would Julius Caesar do?
Me semper rogo, Quid faceret Iulius Caesar?

No, as far as miracles go, this 'J.C.' never raised the dead,
but he certainly lowered a lot of the living
**Immo, si de miraculis agitur, ille 'I Ce' nullos mortuos
ad vitam revocavit, sed tamen multos vivos ad
mortem sane misit**

We're having a prayer breakfast down at the rifle range
**Ientabimus, precatione facta, in campo
manuballistulario**

I am a firm believer in tough hate
Mihi persuasum est odisse acerbe

Do unto others, but do it first
Fac hominibus aliis, atqui fac prius

Blessed are the poor, because they leave so much more
money for the rest of us
**Beati pauperes, quoniam tanto plus pecuniae nobis
reliquis relinquunt**

Blessed are the meek, because we can cut in front of them
in queues
**Beati mites, quoniam istis in ordine stantibus
anteponere nosmet ipsos possumus**

If someone smites you on the cheek, turn the other cheek
and see what kind of a smiter he is with a bloody stump
**Si quis te percusserit in dexteram maxillam tuam,
praebe illi alteram ut possis cognoscere quam fortiter
percussurus sit bracchio truncato cruento**

Love thy neighbors, and to show you really mean it, send
50,000 heavily armed soldiers to knock on their door
and ask in the nicest possible way if they'd like to join
your empire
**Dilige proximos tuos, utque illis ostendas te re vera
diligere, mitte decem legiones quae ianuas pulsent et
quam dulcissime ab illis quaerant, num velint in
tuum imperium recipi**

The theory of evolution is baloney. Everyone knows the
whole universe came out of Saturn's nostrils
**Theoria Darwiniana evolutionis specierum absurda est.
Constat inter omnes universitatem rerum ab naribus
Saturni venisse**

Of course I can speak in tongues, but I prefer Latin

Sane loqui variis linguis possum sicut Apostoli die Pentecostes, sed malo Latine loqui

Let's say grace: O gods, thank you for permitting us to gobble this food the way Caesar gobbled up half of Europe. Amen.

Precemur. O di, gratias vobis agimus, quod nos sinitis hunc cibum sic devorare quo modo C. Iulius Caesar dimidiam partem Europae devoravit. Finis.

Mob Banter
CAVILLATIO SODALIUM

It fell off the back of a truck, capeesh?
De extremo plaustro excidit; comprehendisne mente quod dico?

You got a problem with that, paysan?
Num de hoc dubitas, compagane?

Whatsamatter you?
Quid te sollicitat?

Fuhgeddaboutit
Eice id ex animo

Geddouttahere
Noli mecum nugari

God forbid, a piano should fall on your head
Dii prohibeant ne clavicinium in caput tuum delabatur

New Age Discourse
SERMO NEOMYSTICUS

Meditate on this, pal
Meditare de hoc, amice

Do you know the yoga position where you put your head
between your legs and kiss your ass goodbye?
**Scisne schema gymnosophisticum per quod, capite
inter femora flexo, iubentur basio valere clunes?**

Did a dish of potpourri just catch fire, or did someone
light up a joint?
**Utrum patella florum siccatorum ignem modo
concepit, an aliquis accendit sarcinulam cannabis?**

Man, that shit is potent – I am like totally in the
subjunctive
**Mehercle, illa materia tam valida est ut funditus in
modo subiunctivo sim**

I've got the munchies! Pizza pizza!
Esurio! Libum Neapolitanum!

Hollywood Latin
SERMO LATINUS ACUIFOLIIS

I love it, I love it, I love it!
Id amo, id amo, id amo!

Make the mother the father, change the cat to a dog, and
lose the kid with cancer
**Muta matrem in patrem, converte felem in canem,
amitte puerum cancerosum**

And replace all the love scenes with car chases and set it in
the Hamptons instead of the Civil War
**Substitue autem persecutiones curriles pro episodiis
eroticis, et conloca dramatis actionem in Hamtunis in
vicem temporis Belli Civilis Americani**

Wait, the girl in the copy room hated it!
Siste, puella in scriptorio xerographico fabulam oderat!

I'm putting it in turnaround
Hoc scriptum in purgatorium committo

Pasadena
Praetermitto

You'll never eat lunch in this town again
Numquam in hoc oppido prandebis iterum

Sushi Bar Chitchat
SERMO IN TABERNA IAPONICA PULPAMENTORUM INCOCTORUM MARINORUM

No mackerel, no eel, and no slab of cold egg crud
Mihi nullus scomber, nulla anguilla, nullum frustum ovorum frictorum frigidorum

When I snap apart the chopsticks, do I make a wish?
Estne mos homini findenti virgulas prehensorias aliquod optatum declarare?

What's the deal with the little strip of green plastic with the fringe on top?
Quapropter in catillum poni solet illa taeniola plastica viridis fimbrata?

More tuna, please, and another California roll
Da mihi plus de thunno, sodes, et alterum volumen Californicum

How do you get the little piece of fish to stick to the rice ball?
Quo modo cogitur segmentulum piscis globo oryzae adhaerere?

Are those knives as sharp as they look?
Suntne illi cultri tam acuti quam esse videntur?

You guys make great cars!
Vos vehicula praestantia fabricamini!

Sorry about those atom bombs!
Me paenitet illorum pyrobolorum atomicorum!

Thank you very much!
Vobis plurimas gratias ago!

Computer Language
SERMO LATINUS
COMPUTATORIUS

Download the goddamn file, you bug-ridden piece of shit
Assume plicam damnatam, o tu moles muscaria muscerdarum

If you freeze one more time, you're going straight to the landfill
Si denuo congeles, confestim ibis in fossam purgamentorum

Yeah? Well I've got an error message for you, fuckhead – you're about to be shut down improperly with a sledgehammer
Sicine? Nunc age, tibi nuntium erroris habeo, stuprator – mox improprie sopieris malleolo

Car Talk
DISCEPTATIO DE CURRIBUS

It's a hunk of junk!
Acervus inutilium est!

That car is so ugly, you'd have to put a pork chop on the
backseat to get the dog to ride in it
**Iste currus tam turpis est ut necesse tibi sit ponere
offam porcinam in sede postrema ut persuadeas cani
ut vehatur eo**

You deserve a smack for buying it!
Eum tam imprudenter comparando meruisti alapam!

If the rattle gets too bad, wear earplugs
Nimium si strepat, indue operimenta tuis auribus

Of course you think you can repair it – you're a moron!
Scilicet putas te currum reficere posse – stipes es!

Whatever it is, it's going to cost you five hundred bucks, if
that's what it is
**Quodcumque est, Ioachimicis tibi quingentis constabit,
siquidem est, quod esse creditur**

Try putting it in neutral and pushing it off a cliff

Vide quid eventurum sit si, dinexo ingranagio, currum e scopulo pepuleris

Keep in mind, people in the rearview mirror are even stupider than they appear

Tene memoria, viatores conspectos in speculo retrospicienti stultiores esse quam videntur

And remember, don't drive like my brother!

Et memento, noli agere currum ut frater meus!

B.S.
BUBULUM STERCUS

A coyote whose habitat was destroyed by urban sprawl ate
 my homework

**Suo tractu operto suburbio extenso, canis latrans
 domicilium meum ingressus praescriptum
 domesticum mihi devoravit**

Due to global warming, my homework spontaneously
 combusted

**Orbe terrarum nimium calefacto combustione
 hydrogonanthracum, pensum meum domesticum sua
 sponte flammam concepit**

My homework was seized as evidence by mistake by CIA
 agents in a drug bust at the wrong address

**In domum meam perperam incurrentes, vigiles qui
 exsequuntur usum medicamentorum illicitorum
 nimis studiosi pensum domesticum pro testimonio
 iniuste abstulerunt**

My homework was forcibly recycled by eco-terrorists

**Praescriptum meum domesticum per vim in fibras
 redactum est a sodalitate quae terrore pro Terra
 utitur**

My homework contracted mad homework disease and
  had to be destroyed
**Necesse erat pensum domesticum meum, quod incidit
  in rabiem pensi deleri**

Strict zoning codes enacted by the town board make it
  illegal for me to work at home
**Praescriptis severis de aedificiorum usu decretis a
  decurionibus municipalibus, mihi non licet operari
  domi**

Because of a lack of international standards, the Supreme
  Court ruled 5–4 that I had to stop doing my homework
  immediately
**Normis civitati universae deficientibus, quinque ex
  iudicibus Tribunalis Supremi decreverunt, quattuor
  negantibus, ut pensum statim deponerem**

Small Talk During a Colonoscopy
COLLOCUTIO INTER COLONOSCOPIAM

Now I know how a Muppet feels
Nunc novi quid Manipupa sentiat

Any sign of the trapped miners?
Conspicisne metallicos sepultos?

Are you there yet? Are you there yet? Are you there yet?
Advenistine? Advenistine? Advenistine?

Could you provide me with an affidavit stating that my
head is not, in fact, up there?
**Potesne mihi testimonium impertire adfirmans caput
meum reapse non infixum esse podici?**

Medical Confab

CONFABULATIO CUM MEDICO

I'm afraid I have some bad news, doc
Vereor ne tristem tibi nuntium adferam, medice

I've noticed you have no concept of time – I've been
waiting for over an hour
**Animadverti te nullam notionem temporis habere –
nam plus quam unam horam tibi praestolatus sum**

Your handwriting on prescriptions is totally illegible and
shows signs of dementia
**Chirographum tuum quasi demens in
medicamentorum praescriptis nemo legere potest**

Your manner is oddly distracted
Te geris mirum in modum neglegenter

You have an extremely strange sense of humour
Inusitatissima iocaris

Your fees are insane
Mercedes tuae insanae sunt

I think you have a brain tumour
Puto te tuber in cerebro alere

I'll come by again in a year and see how you're doing
Reveniam ad annum ut cognoscam de valetudine tua

Hang in there!
Perfer et obdura!

Homeland Security
SALUS PATRIAE

I'd open these bills, but I'm afraid they may contain anthrax
**Has epistulas debitorum solutionem poscentes
aperirem, sed metuo ne bacilli anthracis insint**

The bad news is, the Martians have landed and, boy, are
they mean; the good news is they hate Arabs and they
piss gasoline
**Tristis nuntio Martios descendisse et, eheu, truculentos
esse, sed laetus nuntio illos odisse Arabes oleumque
octanum meiere**

If you don't give me this putt, the terrorists win
Nisi mihi hunc puteolum concedis, phobistae vincunt

If I can't get a decent table at a top restaurant on short
notice, the terrorists have won
**Nisi mensam opimam in popina optima extemplo
accumbere possum, phobistae vicerunt**

If you won't sleep with me, the terrorists will have won
Nisi mecum concubueris, phobistae vicerint

Get out the duct tape – I'm about to fart!
Effer fasciam adhaesivam – mox pedam!

Useful Phrases for Barbarian Evildoers
LOCUTIONES UTILES MALEFACTORIBUS BARBARIS

I surrender! Please do not fire your catapult!
Me dedo! Quaeso, noli iacere tela ballista!

There is no anti-Roman sentiment here!
Hic nemo est quin Romam amet!

We love your big chariots, fast food, and violent culture!
Amamus vestras currus immanes, cibum festinanter paratum, et cultum saevum!

We hate our wicked and corrupt leaders!
Odimus duces nostros improbos pravosque!

We welcome you as liberators, not conquerors!
Vos non victores, sed liberatores salutamus!

We never liked that dirty old city – it's so much nicer as rubble!
Istam urbem squalidam senescentem numquam dileximus – confracta, multo magis nobis placet!

If you see anything you like, don't hesitate to take it!
Si quid videtis quo delectamini, agite, capite sine mora!

We'd much rather be ruled by a distant emperor, even if
he's a nitwit!
**Multo malimus ab imperatore remoto regi, etiamsi
frutex sit!**

We'll be sure to let you know if any Huns come this way!
**Curabimus ut sciatis num ulli Hunni appropinquent
hac via!**

Have a really nice epoch!
Sit vobis aetas felicissima!

Game Boy Chatter
HORTAMINA PUERORUM LUDENTIUM ENCHIRIDIIS LUSORIIS

Taste laser death, alien insect scum!
Oppetite mortem lumine amplificato stimulata emissione radiorum, cimices extraterrestriales foedi!

Eat hot lead, Nazi zombie robot commandos!
Vescimini glandibus plumbi candentis, velites nationalisticosocialistici cadaverosi automatarii!

Feel the keen edge of the sword of doom, no-good, stinking, corpse-eating tomb-ghouls!
Sentite aciem acrem ensis mortiferi, o larvae putidae, o bustirapi nefandi!

I am going to programme a simulation of the Roman Empire and rule it unjustly, cruelly, and incompetently!
Mihi est in animo programmare simulationem imperii Romani quam iniuste, atrociter, imperite regam!

Tax the poor!
Impone vectigalia pauperibus!

Bribe the senators!
Corrumpe pecunia senatores!

Rig the elections!
Falle comitia!

Screw minorities!
Defrauda nationes minores in tua civitate!

Pack the courts with obedient dunces!
Stipa basilicas stipitibus obsequentibus!

Arrest protestors on trumped-up charges!
Infer commenta crimina seditiosis apprehensis!

Invade other countries pretty much at random!
Infer forte temere bellum aliis gentibus!

What could possibly go wrong?
Quid nobis infeliciter fieri potest?

Modern Vatican Latin
SERMO LATINUS HODIERNUS IN VATICANO

My patron saint, Miranda, appeared to me in a vision and told me to remain silent

Patrona mea, Sancta Miranda, apparens mihi somnio me iussit tacere

Whom are you going to believe, me or some snot-nosed little boy, no matter how cute?

Utri vos convenit credere? Mihi, an nescio cui puero parvulo muculento, quamlibet pulchellus sit?

Look, these legal fees are putting quite a dent in the old collection plate

En, mercedes iurisperitorum discum eleemosynarium vero vacuefaciunt

What if I say one million Our Fathers and a couple hundred thousand Hail Marys and we just call it even?

Si Orationum Dominicarum decies centena milia recitabo, Salutationumque Beatae Mariae bis vel ter ducena milia, eritne satis?

On the advice of counsel, I have decided to testify in Latin
**Iurisconsultus mihi suasit ut testimonium dicerem
  Latine**

The devil made me do it!
Diabolus me coegit peccare!

Learned Latin
for Lovers
SERMO LATINUS DOCTUS –
AMATORIBUS

I'm only repeating a query that dates back to the
Chaldeans, but may I ask, what is your sign?

**Si modo licet mihi te rogare idem quod antiqui
Chaldaei suas puellas rogare solebant – quo signo
nata es?**

I think it was Pliny the Elder – or was it Pliny the
Younger? – who first pioneered the concept of self-
introduction by way of the purchase of a libation, and it
is really in homage to him that I am moved to offer to
buy you a drink

**Credo Gaium Plinium Secundum Maiorem – aut Gaium
Plinium Caecilium Secundum Minorem – instituisse
ut vir, qui se notiorem puellae facere vellet, ei aliquid
liquoris Lyaei compararet; itaque in
commemorationem illius iuvat potiunculam tibi
praebere**

Cicero phrased it best, and I am merely quoting the
master when I am driven to remark, 'Nice tits.'

**Hoc Marcus Tullius optime verbis expressit, neque
profero alia quam ipsissima verba optimi omnium
oratorum cum adsevero te venustas habere mammas**

III
SERMO LATINUS
ERUDITUS

ADVANCED LATIN

Useful Syntax
SYNTAXIS UTILIS

IMPERATIVE

Futue te ipsum
Go fuck yourself

IMPERFECT SUBJUNCTIVE EXPRESSING A WISH FOR THE PRESENT

Utinam tete futueres
Would that you would go fuck yourself

FIRST SUPINE EXPRESSING A WISH FOR THE PRESENT WITH VERBS OF MOTION

I fututum te ipsum
Go in order to fuck yourself

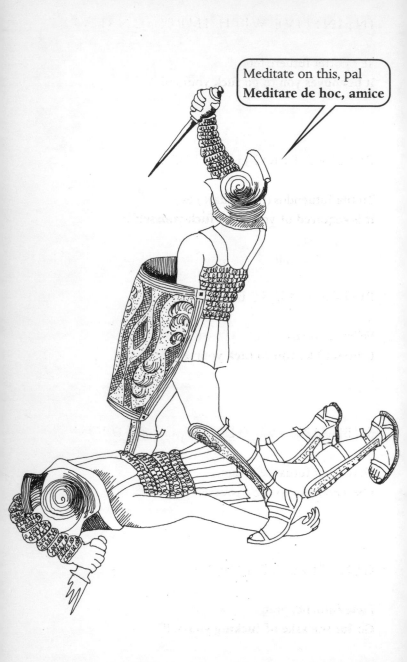

INFINITIVE WITH IMPERSONAL VERB

Te oportet futuere tete
It behooves you to go fuck yourself

PASSIVE PERIPHRASTIC

Tu tibi futuendus (futuendave) es
It is required of you to go fuck yourself

POTENTIAL SUBJUNCTIVE

Velim te futuas
I should like you to fuck yourself

SUBSTANTIVE CLAUSE OF PURPOSE

Te rogo ut futuas te ipsum
I beseech you to fuck yourself

GENITIVE OF PURPOSE

I tete futuendi gratia
Go for the sake of fucking yourself

FUTURE CONDITIONAL, LESS VIVID

Si te futuas, gaudeam
If you should go fuck yourself, I would rejoice

FUTURE CONDITIONAL, MORE VIVID

Se te futueris gaudebo
If you will have gone and fucked yourself, I will rejoice

PRESENT CONDITIONAL, CONTRARY TO FACT

Si te futueres, gauderem
If you were fucking yourself, I would be rejoicing

PAST CONDITIONAL, CONTRARY TO FACT

Se te futuisses, gavisus (gavisave) essem
If you had fucked yourself, I would have rejoiced

FUTURE PARTICIPLE DENOTING INTENTION OR LIKELIHOOD

Tete fututure, te saluto
You who are about to go fuck yourself, I salute you

FUTURE IMPERATIVE

Tete futuito
Make it your policy to fuck yourself

ABLATIVE ABSOLUTE

Te fututo, gaudeo
You having been fucked, I rejoice

. . . you often forget what you were going to say before you get to the verb

. . . saepe quid habeas in animo dicere priusquam ad verbum pervenias, obliviscaris

. . . you think only superstitious sissies are afraid of volcanoes

. . . credas molles superstitiosos solos timere montes Volcanios

. . . you can eat and have sex at the same time

. . . simul cenare et futuere possis

. . . you have ever used a chariot in a bar fight

. . . umquam in taberna curru proeliatus sis

. . . you never make major business decisions without first cutting open a sheep

. . . numquam de negotio magni momenti decernas sine extispicio

. . . your most recent domestic crisis was a slave revolt

. . . discrimen apud te recentissimum tumultus fuerit servilis

. . . you know anyone who married his own mother or was raised by wolves

. . . quempiam cognoscas qui matrem suam in matrimonium duxerit vel sit a lupis alitus

. . . you have a statue of yourself holding a sword in one hand and the severed head of a Belgian in the other

. . . possideas statuam tui, tenentem manu dextra gladium, manu sinistra caput amputatum Belgae

. . . you compliment the chef by throwing up

. . . coquum vomendo in mensam conlaudes

. . . you have a personal poisoner on your staff

. . . unus ex officialibus tuis propriis est venenarius

. . . the only vegetarian you ever met had hooves

. . . numquam phytophagis occurreris nisi ungulatis

. . . your idea of a party animal is a goat

. . . animal convivialissimum arbitreris esse caprum

. . . your car has sword blades welded to its wheels

. . . habeas currum falcatum

. . . there are usually about three hundred other people in the tub when you take a bath

. . . plerumque, cum laveris, adsint in calidario tecum alii fere trecenti

. . . you think it would be really cool to be Greek

. . . putes esse lepidissimum Graecari

. . . you stay home all day if you see a woodpecker over
your left shoulder or hear an owl

**. . . domi maneas totum diem cum post tergum
conspicias a sinistra picum, vel audias bubonem**

. . . you're never surprised to discover that the guy
running the empire is a moron, a pervert, or a lunatic

**. . . numquam admireris te invenire gubernatorem
imperii fatuum esse, vel pravum, vel vesanum**

Restaurant 'Tude
BILIS IN POPINA

My name is Sir – I'll be your customer tonight
Nomen mihi est Dominus – hodie vobiscum cenabo

My sign is, I sign the cheque
Natus sum signo signantis syngrapham

The only thing I wish to know about you is where the hell
you are when I want something
**De te scire volo solum ubi gentium sis cum alicuius
indigeam**

If those entrées are so special, why aren't they on the
menu?
**Si quidem illa fercula tantum praestant, cur in
epularum indice non sunt?**

Exactly how fresh is that pepper?
Quam recenter lectum est hoc piper?

Why do you put it in a mill the size of a war-trumpet?
Quamobrem id ponis in molina tanta quanta tuba est?

This is indeed a very impressive wine list, if you're in the mood for a bottle of grape-flavored rust remover that costs as much as a new sofa

Haec tabula vinorum grandia pollicetur cuicumque sit in animo bibere ex ampulla liquoris qui sapit uvas et solvit ferruginem et stat tanti quanti lectus novus

My compliments to the chef – the empire lost a truly inspired poisoner when he decided to go to cooking school

Summam coquo laudem tribuo – imperium venefico ingeniosissimo privatum est cum ille scholam coquinariam obire statuit

No dessert, thanks, unless it contains the antidote

Benigne, secundam mensam non requiro, nisi antidotum continet

I'd have written in a smaller tip but there is no Roman numeral for a penny

In syngrapha munusculum minus inscripsissem, sed non est littera Romana quae Ioachimici vicesimam significat

I'll be sure to recommend this place to my friends

Zago, zagas, zagat

Winespeak
DICTA ARBITRI VINI

It's an intense chalky white marked by overtones of
turpentine and lead, with a bright, long-lasting finish
**Vinum peralbum cretosum est, resinam terebinthinam
et cerussam redolens, nec sine polimine nitido
durabili**

It's a pointless little red wine with a unique balance of
ignorance and pretension made by an obnoxious
millionaire Napa Valley dilettante for self-important
dumb-lucky dickheads just like him
**Vinum irritum pusillum rubrum est, incomparabiliter
librans ignorantiam suam cum ostentatione, a
quodam Trimalchione Napaensi confectum salaputiis
gloriosis immerito fortunatis, persimilibus sui**

It's a dirt-cheap head-banging screw-top bum wine that I
poured into a leftover bottle with a fancy French label
while no one was looking
**Vappa vilissima est, quae capitis dolores facit, quamque
ex lagona obturamento versatili clausa in lagunculam
reliquam, cui pittacium Gallicum speciosum affixum
erat, transfudi, dum nemo me spectabat**

The Bestseller List
TABULA LIBRORUM
VENDIBILISSIMORUM

*Quick and Easy Decorating Secrets That Let You Turn a Rustic
Hovel into a Charming Country Home without Busting Your
Budget* by Vitruvius

**Artis Ornatus Arcana Per Quae Casa Tua Rustica
Celeriter Expediteque Converti Potest in Villam
Venustam Sine Sumptu Extra Modum Vitruvius
Pollio scripsit**

Eat Right – for that Lean and Hungry Look! by Cassius

**Edi Recte – ut Speciem Macram et Ieiunam Geras
auctore C. Cassio Longino**

*Great-Tasting Hot Meals Your Slaves Can Whip Up in Two
Days or Less* by Cato the Elder

**Edulia Calida Sapidissimaque quae Familia Tua Potest
Parare Duobus Diebus vel Uno M. Porcius Cato
descripsit**

*Cleopatra's Hour-a-Day Bun-Firming Love-Muscle Sexercise
Workout* by Mark Antony

**De Cleopatrae Callipygiana Exercitatione Aphrodisiaca
Per Unam Horam in Singulos Dies Musculorum
Venereorum M. Antonius scripsit**

Letters to My Cat by Pliny the Younger
**Epistulae ad Felem Suam quas C. Plinius Caecilius
Secundus scripsit**

What Colour is Your Catapult? by Frontinus
**Cuius Coloris est Catapulta Tua? Sextus Iulius
Frontinus scripsit**

Oracles Say the Darnedest Things by Livy
**Oraculis Inusitatissima Enuntiantur Titus Livius
scripsit**

Entrail Reading for Dummies by Cicero
Haruspicium Stipitibus Explicat M. Tullius Cicero

Men Are from Troy, Women Are from Greece by Virgil
**E Troia Viri, Ex Graecia Feminae Oriuntur P. Virgilius
Maro scripsit**

*Now You Can Lose Weight without Vomiting with the
Revolutionary Lark's Tongue Diet* by Apicius
**Nunc Adipem Deponere Potes Sine Vomitu per
Diaetam Novam atque Inauditam Quae Linguarum
Alaudarum Esum Praescribit L. Apicius scripsit**

Toujours, Gaul by Julius Caesar
Semper, Gallia C. Iulius Caesar scripsit

Latin for Trekkies

SERMO LATINUS SECTATORIBUS PEREGRINATIONIS ASTRALIS

Our shields are down to 25 per cent and those stupid sparks are coming out of all the control panels!

Scutorum nostrorum potestatis remanet solummodo quarta pars, et istae scintillae ridiculae ex omnibus claviaturis gubernatoriis evolant!

We're being controlled by a subordinating conjunction of time implying purpose or intent

Coercemur coniunctione subiunctiva temporali quae propositum vel intentionem significat

Resistance is futile. Prepare to be assimilated into the subjunctive.

Resistere irritum est. Praeparate vos ad translationem in modum subiunctivum.

It's our only hope. Activate the transitive verbs and engage the ablative of separation.

Hoc sola spes nobis est. Verbis transitivis citis, adhibe casum ablativum separationis.

We're entering the future perfect indicative. We'll only
have one chance to achieve a case shift.

**Intramus tempus futurum perfectum modo indicativo.
Unam tantum occasionem habebimus mutandi
casum.**

We're slipping into the passive. Quick, reroute all available
power to the verb endings.

**In genus passivum labimur. Inmitte cito impetum
omnem quem in promptu habemus in terminationes
verborum.**

We have entered. We shall have entered! Do be entering!

Intravimus! Intraverimus! Intratote!

To be continued . . .

Narratio resumetur . . .

Attack Ads
PRAECONIUM PROCAX CANDIDATORUM

Ask my opponent why he wants to put a tax on Bibles and American flags to buy gourmet meals for convicted murderers

Quaerite a competitore meo cur vectigal Bibliis Sacris et vexillis Americanis imponere velit ad epulas comparandas homicidis condemnatis

Call my opponent and demand that he stop accepting campaign contributions from operators of nursing-home casinos, publishers of pornographic children's books, and owners of Mexican puppy mills

Vocantes competitorem meum poscite ut desinat accipere ad ambitionem alendam dona vel ab eis qui virginibus puerisque libros edunt Sotadicos, vel ab eis qui aleatoria in gerontocomiis apparant, vel ab eis qui catellos in Hispania Nova immodice alunt

Tell my opponent you oppose his plan to sponsor a law forcing Sunday schools to hire unemployed bilingual homosexual drug addicts

Dicite competitori meo vos obstare proposito suo ferendi legem quae cogat ludos Dominicales conducere paedicatores otiosos bilingues narcomaniacos

Business Latin
SERMO LATINUS NEGOTIALIS

I respectfully decline to answer on the grounds that anything I might say would be a bald-faced lie

Recuso reverenter ne respondeam, quia quicquid dicam id sit mendacium impudens

It wasn't all done with smoke and mirrors – there were some bells and whistles, too

Non solum fumo speculisque, sed etiam tintinnabulis fistulisque factum est

It wasn't really a loss, it was a loan, which of course shows up as a profit

Non vero damnum erat sed mutuum, quod scilicet in rationibus existimatur lucrum

I was out of the loop, but I distinctly remember asking if it passed the smell test

Consilii particeps non eram, tamen memini clare me rogare num id insidias oleret

Due to an alien abduction, I have no recollection of anything else during that particular period of time

Quod raptus sum a transaetheriis, omnia quae evenerunt illo tempore de memoria mea exciderunt

I only sold my stock because a gypsy fortune-teller told
me it was an unlucky month for any company with a
vowel in its name

**Omnes partes meas vendidi tantummodo eo, quod
Aegyptia sortilega mihi dixit mensem infaustum esse
cuiquam societati quae vocalem in nomine habet**

Plus which, I needed cash to buy a condominium for my
daughter's hamster

**Mihi autem pecunia opus erat ad domicilium emendum
criceto filiae meae**

I mistook the shredder for a Xerox machine
Discissorem esse Xerographium perperam putavi

Look, let me off the hook and I will rat out every single
person in the whole company

**Age, da mihi veniam ac impunitatem, deferam
unumquemque hominum in societate**

Let the buyer go mad
FURAT EMPTOR

Ministerium consultatorium rerum technicarum tibi
gratias agit quod vocavisti
Thank you for calling tech support

Verisimile est te haudquaquam intellegere quod dicimus;
quid enim?
**You probably don't understand a word we're saying;
but so what?**

Vocatum tuum nullius momenti putamus eumque
neglegemus in ordine
**Your call is of no interest to us and will be ignored in
the order it was received**

Fieri potest ut vocatum tuum subauscultemus vel
transcribamus animi causa
**Your call may be monitored or recorded to provide us
with entertainment**

Omnes auxiliatores nostri nunc emptores alios
furiant
**All of our representatives are currently driving
other customers crazy**

Necesse tibi est morari circa tres dies et dimidiam
**Your approximate waiting time is three and one-half
days**

Preme gullulam primam uti musicam molestam audias
Press one to hear irritating music

Preme secundam ut sonum funis occupati audias
Press two to hear a busy signal

Preme tertiam uti tinnitum sempiternum lineae vacuae
audias
**Press three for the endless ringing of a non-working
extension**

Preme quartam uti statim disiungaris
Press four to be immediately disconnected

Sit iucundus tibi dies
Have a nice day

Jury Duty
OFFICIUM IUDICIALE

I'm hopelessly prejudiced – everyone in this court looks
like a criminal, including the judge

**Opinionem praeiudicatam immutabilem habeo –
omnes in hac basilica mihi videri nefarios esse,
praetore non excepto**

Not fair! Just last month I served as a hooded judge on a
secret military tribunal, but they made me promise not
to tell.

**Iniquum est! Modo proximo mense officio iudicis
cucullati functus sum in tribunali clandestino militari
tamen coactus sum iurare me de eo taciturum.**

I swear to tell the truth, the whole truth, and nothing but
the truth, so help, help me Rhonda

**Iuro sollemniter me dicturum verum, totum verum,
nihil praeter verum, ita me iuvet, iuvet Rhonda**

I think I can tell if someone is guilty just by looking at
them

**Credo me posse diiudicare utrum quis nocens an
innocens sit modo eum spectando**

If it's really, really close and the jury deadlocks, is it okay
to flip a coin?

**Si lis valde dubia sit, sententiis iuratorum paribus,
liceatne nos nummum iactare, 'caput aut navem'
enuntiantes?**

If the guy is obviously guilty, can we just skip the trial and
send him straight to prison under early admission?

**Si reus manifesto sit in culpa, sitne fas nos quaestionem
praetereuntes condemnatum in carcerem confestim
conicere per admissionem subitariam?**

If the gloves don't fit, do we have to acquit?

**Si digitalia non congruant manibus, sitne nobis necesse
reum absolvere?**

Does the jury room have a minibar?

**Estne cubiculum deliberationis instructum cistula
potionum spirituosarum?**

I believe the minimum award in civil cases should be one
million dollars, but if you lose, you get the electric chair

**Mea sententia, causam privatam obtinenti ut minimum
decies centena milia Ioachimicorum addici debent, at
de perdente supplicium ultimum in electrica sella
sumendum est**

I plan to find everyone not guilty by reason of I am
extremely pissed off

**In animo mihi est, iracundiae meae maximae causa,
quemque reum absolvere de crimine**

But in a larger sense, can any of us say that we are truly
  innocent?
**Quod autem ad res universas attinet, ecquis nostrum
  dicere potest se vere innocentem esse?**

No, no! It was me! It was me all along! I did it! I did it and
  I'm glad! Ha-ha, just kidding.
**Minime! Non est! Ego fui! Semper ego! Ego facinus feci!
  Atque gaudeo me fecisse! Hahahae! Tantummodo
  iocabar.**

Stealth Latin
SERMO LATINUS CLANDESTINUS

What you say in Latin
What you say it means
What it really means

Stupra fascino volanti torum pistrinum provolventem
You never cease to amaze me with your deeply insightful remarks
Go take a flying fuck at a rolling doughnut

Quin futuis uxorem tuam foedam?
Why doesn't everyone recognize your genius?
Why don't you go screw your ugly wife?

Velim caput tuum devellere deinde in confinium gulae cacare
I just want to tell you how much I appreciate your constructive criticism
I'd like to rip off your head and take a dump in the hole

Mande merdam et morere
Keep up the good work
Eat shit and die

Propudium parcissimum
I'll get the cheque
You cheap bastard

Carrus exsecrabilis est! Venditor te irrumavit!
What a great car! You got a heck of a deal!
What a piece of shit! You got taken to the cleaners!

Aspice hanc supellectilem vilem. Quale gurgustium est.
Fabulous house – I love your taste.
Look at this cheesy crap. What a dump.

Rotaturne capitulum huius, virus exspuens viride?
Well, now, really, isn't that the cutest baby you've ever
seen?
Does its head spin around and spit green slime?

**Amica tua est originis extraterrestrialis. Si fortuna tibi
faveat, cum astronavem suam ista refecerit, a terra
tuaque vita discedet tam cito quam fulmen ascendit.**
Your girlfriend is a knockout. Talent, beauty, brains – she
has it all.
*She's a space alien. If you're lucky, when she gets her flying
saucer fixed, she'll be out of here and out of your life in a
flash.*

**Amicus tuus expers rationis est. Viculus nescioquis
barone suo privatus est.**
Your boyfriend is a great guy. No wonder you've been
keeping him to yourself.
*He's a total moron. Somewhere there's a village missing its
idiot.*

Speciem scurrae habes. Spectaculum petauristarum bestiarumque nescieGam adesse.

Dynamite outfit! It really looks good on you.

You look like a clown. I didn't know the circus was in town.

Stealth Latin for Golfers
SERMO LATINUS CLANDESTINUS IN LUSU CALEDONIO

Quod fustuarium!
Nice swing!
What a hack!

Salaputium fortunatum!
Great shot!
You lucky fuckhead.

Seligatur clava imprudenter
Be the right club.
Be the wrong club.

Pilula, curre in harenariam et defode te.
Hurry up ball, get some air! Be there!
Get in that bunker and bury.

Vola! Aberra! Egredere praeter terminos!
Stop! Hit something! Stay in play!
Go! Get lost, ball! Go out of bounds!

Immerge te in aquam!
Stay dry!
Get wet!

Decurre ab area leni in gramen densum!
Sit down! Bite!
Run off the green into the rough!

Transili puteolum!
Go in the hole!
Lip out!

Euax!
Aww, too bad!
Hurray!

Bad Latin, the Dirty Dozen
SERMO LATINUS IMPUDICUS: DUODECIM OBSCENA

asshole	*culus, i* m.; *podex, podicis,* m.
balls	*coleus, i* m.;
to be blown & to blow	*irrumo, irrumare* *fello, fellare;* *ligurio, ire;* *(verpam) comedo, esse, edi, estum*
to bugger	*pedico, are*
butt	*clunis, is* m. & f. *(clunes, ium);* *natis, is* f. *(nates, ium);* *puta, ac* f.
cock	*capulus, i* m.; *cauda, ae* f.; *cicer, is* n.; *clavus, i* m.; *cucumis, eris* m.; *falcula, ae* f.; *fascinum, i* n.; *gladius, i* m.; *hasta, ae* f.; *membrum, i* n.;

mentula, ae f.;
peculium, i n.;
radix, icis, f.;
rutabulum, i n.;
sicula, ae f.;
telum, i n.;
verpa, ae f.;
vomer, eris m.

cunt   *aratiuncula, ae* f.;
cunnus, i m.

fart, to fart · *crepitus, us.* m.:
strepitus, us m.;
crepo, crepare, crepui, crepitum;
pedo, pedere, pepedi, peditum;
strepito, are

to fuck   *concumbo, concumbere, concubui, concubitum;*
futuo, futuere, futui, fututum

to jerk off   *frico, fricare, fricui, frictum (fricatum);*
percleo, ire, ivi, ilum;
sollicito, are;
tero, terere, trivi, tritum;
tracto, tractare

piss, to piss   *urina, ae* f.;
meio, meiere, mixi, mictum;
mingo, mingere, minxi, minctum

shit, to shit   *fimus, i* m. & *filmus, i* n.;
merda, ae f.;
stercus, oris n.;
caco, are